Table of Contents

INTRODUCTION

One of the greatest challenges of today is to end hunger and poverty while making agriculture and food systems sustainable. However, providing clean and fresh food for next generation is our main concerns especially for growing global population. The world food production is rising faster than population and per capita consumption increase. Studies reported that in 2050, the world population expects to surpass ten billion people, 34% higher than now. Nearly much of population increase will occur in the developing countries. The high concentration of people has major socioeconomic ramifications, food production, supply and security issues which require closer examination. Also, it will highlight the several problems, challenges and cause to increase the number of hungry and malnourished people. In 2050, additional 60% to 70% global food production will need to feed the more urban and larger population. Aeroponic systems nourish plants with nothing more than nutrient-laden mist. The concept builds off that of hydroponic systems, in which the roots are held in a soilless growing medium, such as coco coir, over which nutrient-laden water is periodically pumped. Aeroponics simply dispenses with the growing medium, leaving the roots to dangle in the air, where they are periodically puffed by specially-designed misting devices. In the 21st Century, alternative food systems are constantly being researched; moreover, aeroponics has the potential to eradicate current commercial food procedures, due to its ease of cultivation and quick crop rotation. Current plant farming techniques are old and out of date.

In aeroponics systems, seeds are "planted" in pieces of foam stuffed into tiny pots, which are exposed to light on one end and nutrient mist on the other. The foam also holds the stem and root mass in place as the plants grow.

CHAPTER ONE

What is Aeroponics

The word Aeroponics is derived from two Latin words meaning aero (air) and ponic (work), air at work.

In other words, the whole plant, roots and all, are suspended in mid air. Simple put the roots are not covered, not buried, not submerged in any form of liquid or matter, they are revealed openly in thin air.

It's so simple and basic. Why do so many complicate the issue? Because, they have their own agenda to make or they want to profit from it. Please, don't be taken by such false advertisement.

Good! We got that out of the way. We will return to the definition later. But for now let's focus on what aeroponics really is.

Grow it fast! Grow it Big!

Aeroponics is the fastest way to grow plants than any other growing method. Aeroponics is the process of growing plants in thin air where its roots are exposed to a misty environment. No soil or aggregate medium is used to support the plant.

Carbon dioxide in the air is necessary for healthy plant growth. However, oxygen is needed for roots to absorb the nutrients that surround them. True aeroponics is conducted in air enriched with micro-droplets of nutrient water.

The Aeroponics system can grow herbs, vegetables and flowers continuously to allow the grower to obtain yields like never before.

Aeroponics is perfect for indoor gardening, grow rooms and greenhouses. However, it has been used successfully for outdoor growing of large or tall plants.

Which Aeroponics are you talking about? High or Low

This opens another issue about aeroponics. There are two types or forms of aeroponic systems. The first one is HPA (High Pressure Aeroponics), and the other is LPA (Low Pressure Aeroponics).

HPAs are considered to be True Aeroponics and was used by NASA to grow vegetables. It also is the most expensive and the most complicated growing system to build. However, HPAs use less resources for plant grow: 98% less water, 60% less fertilizer, and 100% less pesticides (no pesticides), all supported by NASA laboratory studies.

LPAs are lower cost system. LPA systems are the most common used and built by DIYers.

High Pressure Aeroponics is True

The HPA (True Aeroponics) system was revolutionized by NASA in the 1990's by reporting it as the most efficient way to grow plants in space. Studies have shown many benefits of growing plants with aeroponic techniques on both Earth and in space.

HPA systems must operate at a high pressure, normally above 80 PSI, but ideally at 100 PSI. The high pressure is used to atomize the nutrient water through a small orifice (hole) to create water droplets of 50 microns or less in diameter, in other words a fine mist like hair spray.

One micron is one-millionth of a meter. The average diameter of human hair is 80 microns. So we are talking about a really tiny water drop.

HPA also must run on a much accurate time cycle. HPAs might run 1 to 5 seconds on, and then off for three to five minutes. Specific components are required in controlling the timing interval and creating the proper size mist.

The basic components of a HPA are as follows:

1. High-Pressure water pump

2. Pre-Pressurize Accumulator Tank

3. Electrical-Solenoid hooked to an adjustable relay timer

4. Pressure switch

5. Mister nozzles

Low Pressure Aeroponics is Cheaper

LPA systems use a standard magdrive pump couple to some PVC or tubing, and a few miniature sprinkler heads. The water spray from an LPA sprinkler head has large droplets that drown the plant roots.

LPAs generally run the pump 24 hours and 7 days a week, continually wetting the roots. This works well, and are cheap and easy to build. However they are not as efficient as HPA systems.

Also, for this to be truly an aeroponics system the reservoir most be separated from the grow chamber of the plants.

The basic components of a LPA are as follows:

1. High flow water pump

2. Micro sprinklers

Aeroponic systems on the market

Getting back to the definition of Aeroponics: Air at work – This means the plant roots are suspended in mid air.

Simply put the plant roots are not covered, not buried, not submerged in any liquid or matter; they are openly suspended in thin air. So if some or all of the roots are sitting in any liquid, then it's not aeroponics.

Any system using a single container to grow and store nutrients, can't be aeroponics.

Aerogarden is Not aeroponics – Ginger Booth, the Indoor Salad Lady, calls it a glorified nutrient film technique hydroponics system. It's sold on the market alluding it's aeroponics. However, it's just a twisted hydroponic system. The plant roots are submerged in a pool of water. Guess what? It's a single container solution.

Tower Garden is aeroponics LPA style, it's not True Aeroponics. The system drips the nutrient over plant roots in a hollow tube. I like Tim Blank the inventor. Due to the Tower Garden being easy to operate and includes a very supportive network, it has become popular with many gardeners. However, it's overly sold as THE AEROPONIC system which it's not. The Tower is sold as part of a multi-level-marketing company that became successful providing and healthy choices.

Remember, true aeroponics must atomize the nutrient to a fine mist using high pressure.

Why Is Aeroponics Great?

We all know what plants look like in soil and how soil provides mechanical stability. Plants absorb nutrients from the soil mix or as irrigation additives poured onto the soil. Plant roots work against the mechanical resistance of soil and expend energy searching for nutrients and oxygen in the soil. Water in moist soil helps the roots expand and with the absorption process at the root surface.

Hydroponics comes in varying levels where soil is replaced with nutrient in-solution water. Plant roots can be flooded and drained on a cycle, or in DWC hydroponics, permanently submerged in water (Deep Water Culture). Hydroponics offers the advantage of no energy wasted searching for nutrients.

Aeroponic systems are a specialized version of hydroponics where the roots of the plant extend only in air and the roots are directly sprayed with a nutrient water mix (the recipe). The primary difference is the availability of oxygen to the roots. In hydroponics, one has to be sure to supply oxygenated water. Standing water gets depleted of oxygen over time. In aeroponics, oxygen is surrounding the roots at all times. Surplus oxygen accelerates nutrient absorption at the root surface.

Plant support in both aeroponics and hydroponics are provided by the hosting environment. Hydroponic plants tend to be stabilized with hydroton clay balls or coco-coir soil alternatives and flooded or submerged in water. Nutrients for hydroponics are provided in solution in the water. For aeroponics, the roots dangle directly in the air and the nutrient salts are mixed with water and sprayed as a vapor directly onto the roots. This completely eliminates mechanical resistance. Roots can grow and expand their surface area at will.

Oxygen Impact

Oxygen and moisture are key to the process of nutrient absorption in the cycle of photosynthesis. Nutrient salts move through the plant root surface along with water and oxygen to begin the conversion cycle. These nutrients transport up into the canopy level as compounds where photosynthesis uses light energy converting CO2 and nutrient salts into plant growth, while releasing oxygen and water into the air. So the summary is roots need oxygen while the canopy needs carbon dioxide.

The difference in aeroponics vs. hydroponics vs. soil beyond the surplus of oxygen is control. Soil can be very forgiving. Plants in soil will grow naturally at a slow rate as roots extend their way through the soil. Soil can stay moist for extended periods of time as plants grow. Hydroponics and aeroponics accelerate this process by providing nutrients directly to the roots. Hydroponics has the downside that oxygen levels have to be managed over time. Standing water, depleted oxygen, pH levels, and nutrients can trigger algae growth and fungal problems in hydroponics. This requires steady attention. Hydroponic nutrient dosing is normally managed on a batch volumetric level. Everything is mixed at one time, irrigated, and when it runs out, mixed again. Managing nutrient dosage, water acidity levels (pH), and oxygen mix is a complex process in-solution. Providing the same nutrient levels to hydroponic plants across this cycle and a large irrigation area can be a challenge.

Aeroponics supercharges plant growth with a surplus of oxygen at the root surface. When this is combined with sensor technology and dynamic nutrient recipe dosing, plant growth is superior.

Aeroponic nutrient "dosing" can be precision optimized for nutrient dosage, spray time, light synchronization, growth phases, flowering, bloom, and fruiting cycles and pH levels, to maximize results. In a proper clean room environment, aeroponics delivers pure fresh results, with zero pesticides, highest quality flavors, and maximum growth.

Precision Sensors, Advanced Automation Software, & Nutrient Recipes Offer Growth Breakthroughs With Aeroponics!

• Rapid Aeroponic Growth = Yield & Profits

• No Pesticides, No Pesticide Residue = Higher Quality

• Pure Water: No Heavy Metals No Pathogens, No Antibiotics, No Hormones = Just Great Taste!

• Automation Simplifies The Process - No Disruption, More Growing Time = Lower Cost

• Reduce Stress - Plants Start Healthier = No Mechanical Resistance From Soil & Create Greater Yields Faster

• Internal Methods Protected - Proprietary Nutrient Recipes, Irrigation Cycles, & Light Automation = Proprietary Advantage

Root Zone Control

More Oxygen & No Mechanical Resistance From Soil

Unlike standard hydroponic systems where plant roots are typically submerged in water, aeroponic roots hang in the open air with no mechanical resistance from soil. This enables the roots to grow with abandon to support much larger foliage, bloom, & fruit growth in the canopy.

Dangling roots not only absorb essential minerals from the nutrient spray solution, but this also allows increased oxygen intake to fuel respiration.

This accelerates growth +40% more than in soil, and adds the benefit of greatly reducing nutrient usage (-70%) & water usage (-90%) through scheduled spray-recycling.

Aeroponic History - The Beginning

Aeroponics International's patent for an Aeroponic method and apparatus, developed by Richard Stoner, Founder and President, for greenhouse and nursery crop production. It utilizes an enclosed pulsed application of a hydro-atomized nutrient mist for rapid propagation of plants from cuttings. This Aeroponic technology was originally marketed in 1983 by Genisis Technology, of Boulder, CO. There are over 1,500 installations of the Genisis Aeroponic technology worldwide. Stoner left Genisis in 1986 and acquired the patent rights in 1988.

Aeroponic System Advancements

The original Genesis Aeroponic System has been significantly improved and redesigned for multi-crop production by Stoner since 1989. The improvements included virtually replace in-vitro and greenhouse mini tuber and crop production.

Micro propagation specialists and other plant scientists who have observed this "new generation" of Aeroponic rapid plant biotechnology, named RPB by Aeroponic International, concur that it represents a novel and totally new approach to crop production and research. For example, the implications for the potato industry utilizing RPB is expected to be 600% to 1400% more productive per sq. ft. compared to current tissue culture/greenhouse micro propagation.

A Deep Look at Aeroponics

Aeroponics is actually a subset of the hydroponic system. However, with the hydroponics method, plants use water as the growing medium while aeroponics uses no growing medium at all. This technique was invented during the 1940s and since then, many researchers have added to the theory and application of this method. Aeroponics is considered one of the best methods to grow plants in a soil-free environment and the need for this method has been growing due to a clear need for a more convenient way to grow plants.

In the aeroponic system, plants are not contained in any solid material such as Rockwool or soil. Instead, plant roots are hung in the air in a grow chamber in a closed-loop system. The roots are sprayed with nutrient-rich water or fine, high-pressure mist containing nutrient-rich solutions at certain intervals.

This makes aeroponics a more advanced form than the hydroponic wicking systems, deep water culture, and other types

As all plants need nutrients, the organism will spend a valuable amount of energy growing roots to find these pockets of nutrients in the soil for flower formulation and growth. With hydroponics and aeroponics, nutrients are instead delivered straight to the roots.

Compared to regular hydroponic plants, the plants tend to grow faster and absorb more nutrients because the roots are exposed to more oxygen. Also, there are fewer threats of diseases around root zone disease because there's no place for debris or pathogen to reside.

However, you need to be aware of the fact that aeroponic system chambers are constantly wet with nutrients spray which is convenient for harmful bacteria and fungi to develop. Therefore, it is important to clean and sterilize these misters before using, and occasionally take out and keep these chambers treated with the hydrogen peroxide solution, which can be purchased at any quality hydroponic store.

How Does The Aeroponic System Work?

In the aeroponic system, plants are usually inserted into the platform top holes on top of a reservoir and placed within a sealed container.

Due to no root zone media for plants to anchor in, you need to prepare a support collar that will hold stems in place. These collars must be rigid enough to hold plants upright and keep the roots in place but flexible enough to allow room for roots to grow.

The pump and sprinkler system creates vapor (which is a hydro-atomized spray mixture of water, nutrients and growth hormones) out of the nutrient-rich solution and sprays the mist in the reservoir, engulfing the dangling plant roots and absorbed by them. This spray provides the exact amount of moisture which stimulates the plant's growth and allows it to develop turgidly.

The timer supplies the timed spray intervals and duration for the plants. Some people think that growing plants in aeroponic system would be frailer compared to hydroponics. But that's not true. The secret of aeroponic system all lies in the amount of oxygen exposed to the roots without a root zone media limiting it.

Thanks to this, the plant roots will develop rapidly and grow in a moist air-rich environment. If you want to see their development rate, just lift up the growing chamber to see how they are growing.

Types of Aeroponic Systems

Low-pressure Aeroponics (LPA)

This is the most commonly used aeroponic type used by most hydroponic hobbyists due to its ease to set up, availability at any hydroponic shop, and low cost.

Low-pressure creates droplet size much different from the high-pressure aeroponic system.

What you need for this system is just like any hydroponic system – a pump strong enough to move the water onto the sprinkler heads to spray water around the plant root zone.

High-pressure Aeroponics (HPA)

This type of Aeroponics is more advanced and quite costly to set up as it would require specialized equipment. So they are often used in the commercial production rather than home growers.

The HPA must run at very high pressure to atomize water into tiny water droplets of 50 microns or less.

This system creates such a fine droplet size that create more oxygen for the root zone than the LPA, making it the most efficient system among all aeroponic types.

Ultrasonic fogger Aeroponics

Ultrasonic fogger Aeroponics, or commonly called fogponics, is another interesting type of Aeroponic system.

As the name means, growers would use an ultrasonic fogger to atomize water into super small droplets of water. These are very tiny and you will see it in the form of fog.

Though plants roots find it easier to absorb water in tiny size, there's little moisture in the fog created, and when running over time, it can easier create the salt that can clog these foggers than other Aeroponic types.

For more details about this system, please refer to our post about fogponics.

Which plants to grow?

You can use this system to grow nearly any type of plants and cultivars such as vegetables, nursery stock, houseplants, and bedding. Hundreds of species of plants have been tested and grown successfully by commercial greenhouse owners, researchers and nursery operate using this technique.

Tools needed

What you will need:

• A reservoir/container to hold the nutrient solution

• Nutrient pump

• Mist nozzles

• Tubing to distribute water from the nutrient pump to the mister heads in the growing chamber

• Baskets to suspend plants

• Enclosed growing chamber for the root zone

• Watertight containers for the growing chamber where the plant's root systems will be

• Timer (preferable a cycle timer) to turn on and off the pump

You can purchase these tools at the local gardening/hydroponic supply store or online.

It's quite easy to understand how an aeroponic system works. The purpose of the plant roots hanging in mid-air is to get them exposed to oxygen as much as possible. The high volume of oxygen exposure will stimulate their growth and help them grow faster than they would in the soil, which is a very important benefit of this type of system. This can be seen in the massive root growth of the plants. It has also been proven that this technique increase crop yield X10 compared to using soil. Not only will you be able to collect healthier plants but also grow more crops per year.

No growing media is needed with aeroponics. You can use baskets or closed cell foam plugs (compress around the plant's stem) to suspend the plants. These tools fit in the small holes on top of the growing chamber. In the growing chamber, the mist nozzles will spray the nutrient solution to the plant roots at short intervals. This regular spray has benefits of keeping the roots moist and provide the nutrients they need.

The growing chambers should be airtight and light proof (to prevent the root zone being penetrated by lights and make algae cannot thrive). It must allow air to get in for the growth of plant roots but you also don't want pests to get in or water to spill out. The chamber needs to be able to hold in the humidity as well. The ultimate factor which creates a successful aeroponic system is a balance of plenty of moisture, nutrients and fresh oxygen that you can provide to the roots.

Finally, a major factor which contributes to the success of this system is the water droplet size. A fine mist would create much faster-growing and bushier roots. These roots also have more surface area to absorb the oxygen and nutrients compared to those sprayed with small streams of water from small mist nozzles. This will also mean faster-growing plant canopy.

Pros and Cons

Pros

Benefits of aeroponics include:

• Maximum nutrient absorption for plant roots due to no growing medium

• Massive plant growth because plant roots are exposed to oxygen 24/7. This promotes healthy and fast-growing plants. The mist used on the roots can also be sterilized to prevent plant diseases.

• Higher yields

• Considerably fewer nutrients and water used on average compared to other systems because of higher nutrient absorption rate. You can help the environment by using less water and human labor

• Mobility. You can move around easily plants or even the whole nurseries as all you need is to move the plant from one collar to another

• Little space required. You don't need a lot of space to be able to set up this system. Plants can be added up one on top of each other. With this type of modular system, you can maximize the use of limited space.

• Easy system maintenance because there is no growing medium used. However, you need to disinfect the root chamber regularly, and periodically the irrigation channels and the reservoir

• System can be cleaned easily

• Easy to replace old plants with new ones

• Great educational value. Adults and kids can use this system to grow pet plants and learn a great deal about plants without needing to get their hands dirty.

Cons

• Besides many great advantages, aeroponics also has the downsides that cannot be overlooked such as:

• Require constant attention with pH and nutrient density ratio because this system is sensitive. Understanding what is the right ratio and applying this concept may be difficult for beginners and can only be attempted by those who are more familiar with such systems.

• The cost for initial set up can be high, which can be many hundreds of dollars each

• Require constant supervision

• Susceptible to power outages. You will have to water your plants manually if this happens.

• Require technical knowledge as it one of the most technical to set up. As there is no soil to absorb the excess nutrients, you need to have a good knowledge about amounts of nutrients required by the plant roots

• Dependence on the system. An aeroponic system is made of mist nozzles, high-pressure pumps, and timer. If one of these breaks down, your plants will die easily.

• Require regular disinfection of the root chamber (a common disinfectant is hydrogen peroxide) to prevent root diseases.

• Microorganism can be introduced to plant roots through water.

In conclusion, the best benefits of aeroponics are the massive plant's growth and higher yields compared to other systems. However, these advantages also come with a cost. The price to set up the system is quite expensive and it also requires technical expertise as well as advanced knowledge (about pH and nutrient density ratio) for this special kind of plant cultivation. If you are a beginner in the domain of growing hydroponically, I would say really weigh the pros and cons and choose the best system that you think will work for you at this stage.

Everything You Need to Know for Maximum Plant Yields

Live in an apartment and share a garden? Or lack the space in your own backyard to grow the plants and veggies you'd like to? With aeroponics, you can grow more with less space and indoors too.

Even better news, the systems need far less watering because they're closed-loop so you're recycling unused nutrient-enriched water with delivery time controlled.

Let's just say, if you've been doing any research into hydroponics, aeroponics will most certainly be on your list of get-to-know hydroponics systems.

That's because of all six types, (Wick, Deep Water Culture, Nutrient Film Technique, Ebb and Flow or Flood and Drain systems and Drip Systems are the other five types of hydroponics) aeroponics, although the most technical of all types, will get the best results – every time! That's guaranteed.

There's a reason for that. It's because there's no growing medium used whatsoever.

This begs the question...

How Do The Plants Grow Using Aeroponics?

And that's the part you need to understand before you invest in an aeroponic system because there's quite a few parts required for the technical set up that make it work.

If any component stops functioning as it should, your plants will die fast. That's why you need to understand what's happening under the hood – so to speak.

Understanding How an Aeroponic System Works

The setup of an aeroponic system needs quite a few components for healthy plant root growth. Up top, the only thing the plants need is light. Beneath the surface is where a lot is happening, starting in the reservoir.

You take care of the system, it in turn takes care of the plant roots and they, in turn, provide the nourishment the plant needs for healthy growth and tastier greens, tomatoes too even.

Here are the components that go into a properly functioning aeroponics system:

The Reservoir

This is where all your water and the nutrient solution will be stored. It's a closed-loop system, meaning whatever the plants don't absorb, gets dropped back into the reservoir to be re-sprayed until the plant roots absorb the water solution.

The plants are never submerged in the water though. They're suspended in air using net cups as grow chambers.

Water/Nutrient Pump

Secured to the base of the reservoir is a water pump that's used to pump the water through the piping to the misting nozzles.

Repeat Cycle Timer

The repeat cycle timer is used to control the amount of water dispersed in the reservoir. If you research the recommended cycle times, you'll find growers having success with a misting cycle of one minute on and five minutes off, and others having similar successes on misting for 15-seconds and then off for up to five minutes.

There are no hard and fast rules as to what frequency you set your misting intervals. The important part is that you do set it, because otherwise, the roots will be drenched.

Your best bet is to test every new plant when you start out because the best cycle is the one that lets the plant roots nearlydry out before hitting them with another burst of atomized water.

Misting Nozzles

Different aeroponic systems will have a different number of misting nozzles used inside the chamber. These are an important part of the set up as the smaller the water droplet sprayed through the mister, the better the plant roots can absorb it.

A study by NASA research found that the best range is between 5 and 50 microns for the water droplets, which is the generally accepted standard for a high pressure aeroponics system. The finer the droplets the better the plants can absorb it.

Net Cups / Grow Chambers

Separating the plant roots from the plant tops is done using a lid with precisely cut holes to insert net cups that are used as grow chambers. These cups are inserted through the lid and sealed with (usually) a Styrofoam collar that provides both support for the stems and acts as a water barrier to keep the water contained in the reservoir.

All aeroponic systems have the same components and work the same way, but there are different types…

The Different Types of Aeroponics Systems

Low Pressure Aeroponics (LPA) Systems

An LPA system is the most common setup for home growers because of its cost-efficiency. They're also the most widely available in a variety of places, not limited to hydroponic specialist suppliers.

It is possible to make your own LPA system using PVC for the piping, attaching misters to them and using a fountain or pond pump secured to a reservoir.

You don't need a special pump for an LPA system. What you do need is enough pressure to create a mist in the reservoir.

The problem with finding the right pump for a DIY setup are that pond and fountain pumps don't tend to have a PSI rating. Instead, it's GPH (gallons per hour) and head height.

The head height is more important when choosing a good submersible pump for an LPA system because the higher the head height is, the more pressure is needed to pump the water up 'til it reaches the misters.

You just need to be sure your reservoir is tall enough to accommodate the head height.

For best results, each spray should be angled upwards to spray above the roots and have each spray from the nozzles overlap slightly. You want the spray to create a fine mist and then the water to run from the top of the plant roots, then trickle down and drop back into the reservoir.

What you don't want to do is angle the sprinklers to direct the water straight at the roots. That would drench them and likely drown them resulting in what some aeroponic growers term as soakaponics because the roots get soaked rather than misted.

Depending on the size of container you're using, you could have just three sprinklers, or for larger setups, six or more sprinklers attached.

Several things factor into your water pump to get an ideal mist within the reservoir.

1. The head height because the pressure needs to be forceful enough to travel up the piping to the misters.

2. The more GPH the pump can push through the system to the head height required, the higher a pressure you'll get.

3. The number of misters used will affect its efficiency because with each mister, there's going to be a slight drop in pressure.

Always remember that with a low pressure aeroponic system, you need to use the two ratings. GPH and head height.

And remember this part…

Whatever you think you need, go higher because you can always decrease the water pressure but you can never increase it without upgrading to a more powerful pump.

High Pressure Aeroponics Systems (HPA)

HPA systems are superb for commercial growers but a really costly setup for aeroponics hobbyists and home growers, so most likely unsuitable, unless you're farming. This type of setup can really only be described as the commercial farming method of the future.

To get a peek into how growing is changing to have farms produce fresh vegetables in city centers, check out this video showing a super hi-tech aeroponics farming system in action…

In the 90's, that would've been sci-fi. Today, it's happening.

As you can see, using HPA systems is extremely technical and you can just imagine the cost it would be to set up a farm like this, which is why it's only suited to commercial growers needing to grow more per harvest and get more yields per year.

A general HPA system pump will start with a range 60 to 90 PSI. The more powerful the pump, the finer the spray. For a professional grade setup, you'd be looking at a pump capable of delivering a steady flow of 100 PSI.

Regulating the frequency is where problems set in because these are running 24/7, so you can expect the pump to need replacing more frequently. And that's just to water up to a half dozen plants. When you get into the hundreds, you're then looking at a far higher cost for misters, pumps and tanks.

To extend the life of an HPA pump, a pressurized accumulator tank is used in a professional HPA system. Using an accumulator tank, there's water and pressurized air used so that the pump doesn't have to work as hard, and to maintain a steady PSI.

Due to the high cost of setting up an HPA system, there's no use for them for home growers. There suited to urban farming as they are capable of producing far more yields per harvest and more harvests per year.

It's the HPA system that focuses on getting minuscule water droplets of under 50 microns. Low pressure systems won't produce as small of water droplets, but there will still be a fine mist created by the pump and the sprinkler heads.

Fogponics

Fogponics is a more recent advancement in aeroponics that really takes things to another level. Instead of your plant roots being suspended in the air and sprayed with a fine mist, a fogponics system doesn't use a pump; it uses ultrasonic technology.

It's a disc that's submerged in the water and vibrates at extremely high frequencies that turns the water into a gas form getting water micron sizes down to just one micron and often less.

To really comprehend how small that is, one micron is equal to 1 millionth of a meter. In inches, it's 0.00004."

For the purposes of this book, we're going to be focusing on the setup most suited to home growers – the Low Pressure Aeroponics System because they're the most affordable to set up and use, while getting a healthier grow using no growing medium.

You just need to know how to go about doing that.

How to Work with a Low Pressure Aeroponics System

Let's talk Temperatures

The ideal temperature for any hydroponic reservoir is best maintained between 65oF and 80oF.

The most likely problem you'll be faced with temperature is it dropping and that's often related to the transfer of coldness from concrete floors such as your aeroponics system being setup in the garage or basement.

If you find the temperatures dropping below 65oF frequently, an aquarium heater with a thermostatic regulator should be used to maintain a higher temperature.

If the reservoir temperature is constantly too cold, it will slow down the plant growth. In addition, nutrient solutions added to the water in the reservoir will lose some of their effectiveness.

If on the other hand, you find your temperatures on the rise, which is more likely to happen in the summer months, you may want to use a reservoir chiller instead of the heater – if just turning the heater off doesn't lower the temperature enough.

Ph Level Consistency With Aeroponics Systems

The pH levels are super important in every hydroponic system. The reason being, the mist sprayed around the chamber cannot deliver everything a plant needs to grow. As the roots are suspended in air, there's plenty of oxygen going to be available.

In addition, the cycling of the water misters will create a constant humid environment, getting close to 100% humidity constantly, which is one of the main reasons aeroponics is so effective at growing robust plants.

However, in addition to the oxygen, there's essential minerals the plant is going to need that water alone cannot provide.

These include the essentials of:

• Calcium

• Nitrogen

• Phosphorus

- Potassium

- Magnesium

- Sulfur

The above are the main nutrients that need to be added to the water solution using a plant nutrient feed specifically designed to be used with aeroponic systems so that the roots can get all the nourishment they need for healthy growth.

In addition to added nutrition for the plants, there's the issue of pH, which is a measurement of acidity.

This needs to be just right for each plant. Deionized/distilled water has a neutral pH of 7, but the ideal pH for aeroponic systems leans more on the acidic side of the pH spectrum, requiring a pH of 6.

This doesn't need to be exact, so long as it stays above 5.0 and below 7.0, the roots will do okay.

A pH of 6 is ideal.

It's also worth noting that a lot of plant watering advice emphasizes rainwater as being preferential. That it is. But, you also need to know that not all rainwater has the same pH, or nutrient value because of environmental factors.

Someone living rurally will have cleaner rainwater than someone living in Massachusetts, which has the highest rainwater acidity(pH of 4.1) of 15 states East of the Mississippi (go figure). On average, rainwater is slightly acidic with a pH of 5.6, but that will vary by region.

There are a few ways to test your pH levels with the most accurate being a digital pH meter. The cheapest method is just to use paper strip tests, but you will need to consistently monitor the pH of your water, so in the long run, it's more cost effective to use a digital pH meter.

The other method is to use liquid pH tests. The digital meter is a one-off cost that you can buy once and use repeatedly.

As a LPA system is closed-loop, the water will recycle until the plant roots absorb it. Eventually, the reservoir will need topped up and when you do that, since regular water is more acidic than is preferred for aeroponics, you'll need to use pH adjusters to maintain the consistency.

You can find a pH up and down solution on Amazon.

Using these, you can get your water and the liquid plant feed to the optimal pH of 6.0 and maintain it throughout the grow cycle of each of your plants.

Monitoring EC levels in Your Reservoir

EC stands for Electrical Conductivity and it can tell you a lot about how your plant is growing. Not just what's in your reservoir, but how your plants are using what's available.

Plants are smart creatures. They only absorb what they need. In warmer months, they may take in more water than they do any other nutrients. When the temperatures are cooler, they can take in more of the nutrient solution than they do the water.

Because of this, if your water temperatures aren't maintained at a consistent level, you can find the pH levels alter, especially if your plants take in more water than the nutrients in the water.

When plants take in more nutrients than they do water, you could find leaf-burn becomes an issue. If on the other hand, more water is being absorbed than the nutrients, it's going to slow down the plant's growth rate.

Plants grow more healthily and faster when the EC is maintained at a consistent level. If during a cycle, you find the EC readings are lower than before, then the plant isn't taking in enough nutrients or the solution you're using isn't strong enough. When the EC readings go higher, the nutrient solution is too strong and would need diluting.

Now, the tricky part is keeping the pH and EC consistent because the readings will alter every time you refill the reservoir due to the water starting out acidic before nutrients are added.

EC readings should be taken daily to make sure it stays the same and when they aren't, nutrients should be added or the water diluted. Once a week or up to a fortnight, the reservoir should be cleaned and refilled with the right dilution of nutrient solution.

The reason being, if you don't, different minerals such as copper and zinc can accumulate in the tank causing deficiencies.

Regular cleaning of the tank is a preventative measure to keep your grow healthy. During the week if there are changes, that's when pH balancers (pH up and pH down solutions) can be used to tweak the nutrient solution being sprayed through the misters.

Just like the pH digital meters, you can use EC meters to measure the conductivity levels.

Now, because nutrients are delivering minerals into the water, it's going to create salt and this is where you really need to maintain your system because if you don't, the misters will get clogged causing the pump to work harder than it needs to.

Eventually, the entire system can be compromised because when there's too high a salt level, it can clog your pipes and sprinklers and stop delivering any nutrients to your plants.

If that does happen, because the roots are suspended in air relying on oxygen, humidity and a constant supply of nutrient-enriched water, a failure can see plants die fast.

These aren't like any other growing method where you can be lax with watering. Once the water stops being pumped effectively, the plants are compromised and often can be ruined. That's why they need a lot of monitoring.

Not so much care, but more about keeping an eye on your readings to spot potential problems before they become a problem.

Different plants have different nutritional needs. If you know the EC range for the type of plant you're growing, all you need to do is keep an eye on the readings to keep the conductivity within that range.

For a sample of common plants grown using aeroponics, there's a handy table at GrowthTechnology.com showing a list of target EC ranges for a variety of plants.

Aeroponics Troubleshooting

When you're growing with aeroponics, there's not much you can do manually to treat plant problems because everything is entirely reliant on the system working properly.

Any issues of plant growth, fungi appearing on plant foliage or roots, or even leaf burn, will be because of an issue with your system.

The most common problems with aeroponics are:

Pump malfunctions

Meet your worst nightmare. To put this in the simplest terms, don't skimp on your water pump. Cheap pumps really are nasty with an aeroponic system because the life of your crops relies on this working.

Inside the reservoir tank is close to 100% humidity level – when the pump is working. The water pump is the reason for high humidity. When that stops working, humidity drops fast.

Combine the fast humidity drop along with the fact the pump won't be able to spray any nutrients to the plant, the plant roots are then starved, which is why there's a likelihood of your plants dying if the pump packs in.

The life of your plants relies on the water pump working. The instant it stops, there's a serious problem.

Blocked nozzles

This is an easy one to miss and it's also an easy fix. You see, with all the nutrients in the water being sprayed through the nozzles, those minerals will accumulate salt. Eventually, the salt molecules can accumulate in the pipes, reaching the nozzles at which point they'll block it.

A partial blockage will slow down the misting, whereas a full nozzle blockage will stop any mist being sprayed. For that reason, it's best to regularly check your nozzles are working as they should be.

If they aren't, the only solution you need is isopropyl – aka, rubbing alcohol. Just rub it over the nozzles and it'll get to work breaking down the salt molecules and getting your nozzles unblocked fairly quickly.

Multiple Problems with bacteria and fungi – The One Solution Fix

If you've done any research into the pros and cons of aeroponics, you'll no doubt be aware of bacteria and fungi being of a higher probability than any other growing method.

Well, that's just not true. What is fact is that all the conditions bacteria and fungi need to grow and spread rapidly are present in the reservoir of an aeroponic system. Warm temperatures and a humid environment.

The truth is, there's no more bacteria or fungi concerns with aeroponics other than one and that's Pythium Root Rot. The only reason is because the Pythium disease has a spore that can swim, meaning once it's present in your reservoir, it's going to infect all the water, and be dispersed onto the plants with every spray of the jets.

There's only one thing you can do here and that's prevention because if you do get disease ridden water, your plants will have seen their day.

Hydrogen Peroxide is the solution to fixing all the concerns to do with bacteria and fungi and that's because on contact, it'll eradicate it.

It also brings a new problem to the table and that's the fact it's so strong it can kill your plants, so while you're trying to protect your crops, you could actually risk killing them yourself.

You need to get the dilution part just right, which is even trickier than you'd imagine because the majority of hydrogen peroxide suppliers already dilute what they sell to you.

Food grade is the best you can use since most of your plants will be of the editable type. That's 35% and there's very few manufacturers certified to supply this high a grade of hydrogen peroxide.

The recommended amount of peroxide to use in your reservoir is 3% per gallon to last up to four days. If you're working in liters, it's just 3ml per 1 liter of water. Remember to use the 3% peroxide solution.

At this concentration, your plants will be protected against a variety of bacteria, pests and viruses.

Maintaining Your Aeroponic System

The reservoir is where you need to pay the most attention to for maintenance but don't neglect your grow room.

Two words to remember to grow healthy crops with aeroponics are "sanitize and sterilize."

1 – Sanitize

Everything around your grow room needs to be kept clean, dust free and, and free of anything that's going encourage any bacteria growth. For cleaning, treat your grow room as your kitchen. If anything is spilled, clean it up.

For your plant foliage, you'll want to keep those healthy by trimming off dead leaves, maintaining the temperatures and ensuring the right amount of light is reaching the plant foliage.

2 – Sterilize

The key area to keep sterile is your reservoir. You'll also have the irrigation system (piping delivering the water) to keep sterile, ensuring there's not too high a salt build-up that could block nozzles and decrease the system's efficiency.

For this, hydrogen peroxide is the best solution you can use to keep your reservoir sterile while it's operating. Between grows, that's a different matter that's addressed by a cleaning flush.

A cleaning flush will involve completely sterilizing the system using bleach or similar cleaning agents. A scrubbing brush is best used to make sure you're getting into every crevice within the reservoir.

Once you've thoroughly cleaned what you can, then run the system with a diluted bleach solution so that the piping, and the jet nozzles get sterilized too.

Once your flush is done, you need to get rid of any chemicals you used to clean it by running the system with just water. Let the water get rid of any lingering chemicals then let oxygen do its part to dry everything before you put it to use again with your next grow.

Whilst the reservoir is the key area to keep sterile, any equipment you're using such as pruners should also be sterilized before using on your plants.

Just one snip with a pair of dirty pruners could introduce plant pests or diseases, such as using the same pruner on outdoor plants then snipping one of your plants in your aeroponics system with those before sterilizing them.

Maintaining your aeroponic system is easy when you know why you're taking each step you take. You're keeping your grow room/area clean and tidy (sanitized) to prevent pests from being attracted to the area or airborne pathogens to be introduced that could affect your system and plants.

Sterilizing all the parts in the reservoir and the tools you use to tend to your plants is being proactive instead of reacting to plant diseases, common pests or any viruses.

Small Aeroponics System

Having a small aeroponics system at home can be an educative and also an interesting way to grow plants. You will need a small sized board and water sprayers and timer for the maintenance of the system.

Aeroponics is the method of growing plants without using soil. In this method the seeds are germinated using coil like material or wool and then the plants are suspended in air. The top and the bottom of the plant are exposed, and they are sprayed with nutrient rich water to grow.

In order to make a home based aeroponics system you will need a bucket, an aquarium pump, and if you have a garden hose pipe or tube. A small part of the pipe is enough. Make a nutrient solution or you can buy the readymade solution. Tube inlets will have to be drilled with several holes at equidistant. The tube then is wrapped around the container, starting from the bottom and ending at the top. And, the container is then plugged or closed at one end. The plants will need to be watered or sprayed with nutrients until the roots start to hang out of the container.

The aquarium pump keeps pumping the nutrients from the container in small and consistent quantities. However, you need to keep refilling the nutrient solution. That is the only disadvantage with the homemade system. The container can also use a square transparent box, and it can be connected with a pump and sprayer. You can watch the plant progress in this method.

CHAPTER TWO

BUCKET AEROPONICS

Aeroponics system doesn't require any use of soil and their roots are suspended in the air so that they can receive their goal for the oxygen. They even don't require any growing media. They use generally less water as compared to other types of hydroponics methods. It is also one of the most efficient low labourtypes of farming methods.

Here is the list of plants you can grow with the

Aeroponics System.

Here is the list of the plants you can grow by yourself with the Aeroponics System of farming method.

- Eggplant

- Lettuce

- Watermelon

- Broccoli

- Beets

- Onions

- Cucumber

- Cauliflower

- Cabbage

- Grapes

- Peas

- Peppers

- Potato

- Radish

- Basil

- Ginger

- Rosemary

- Sage

- Oregano

- Mustard

- Ginger

- Mint

We hope that with help from this list you can understand how good and underrated the technique of hydroponic farming method is.

Advantages of the Aeroponics System.

1. Crops can be harvested without the use of soil.

2. Reduced labor costs.

3. Reduce the risk of plant disease due to pest infestation.

4. Roots problem is not a big issue anymore.

5. Roots are provided better exposure with oxygen.

6. No need to immerse roots in the water.

7. Offers much more control.

How to set up a homemade Aeroponics System.

There are two types of Aeroponics System we are to discuss here, one is the single bucket aeroponics system and another one is the multi bucket aeroponics system. Single bucket is for new farmers or for the starters and the Multi Bucket is for the small scale farmers. Some of the tools mentioned can be bought at the nearest gardening markets. You can, also, always opt out for online shopping. Amazon provides you with everything you need. We are going to set up a homemade aeroponics system.

Single-Bucket System Aeroponics Kit

• 1 big plastic planter or a pot without holes.

• 1 small and round flower pot which doesn't touch the planter's ground.

• 1 garden hose of 3 to 7 feet long.

• 1 "T" hose.

• 1 water pump for the aquarium.

• 1 bag full of Clay Pebbles.

• 1 outlet timer for timing the pump.

The time you'll need for making this is about 30 minutes for a single plant and will cost you about $70.

3. The garden hose needs to be cut into two pieces. One piece is for the filter, and one for the "circle" dripper. You will need to drill the small holes in the bottom of the pot, and one large hole for the hose.

4. Put the garden hose used for the pump into the large hole. The second piece of the garden hose will be used to connect both ends to the "T" fitting. Use any type of rubber tube in a place of the hose.

5. Drill cca. 30 smaller holes into the "circle" hose. It should let water to drip down.

No need to drill the holes too big, as the water will need to dispense all around the circle. Drill one hole in the bottom planter, so the pump cord can come out if you desire.

6. Now, you need to connect one end of the hose to the pump outlet and fill the bottom planter with water. Set the pump inside. After dropping into the flower pot and feeding the hose up and through, connect it to the "circle" water dripper. The pump should be at the bottom of the large planter. It needs to have water in the bottom.

7. Fill the flower pot with the Clay Pebbles you have. Then place your seedling down in the hydro balls.

When you finish everything, you can turn the pump on. See the water dripping from the hose.

Let the water drip, and watch your plants grow. Plug the pump for the aquarium into an outlet time. Set as you think is needed.

Note: daily check the level of water inside the bottom planter, and refill if needed.

Multi-Bucket System

Tools:

• 3 x Five-gallon buckets.

• 3 x Grommets 3/4".

• 5 Feet of plastic hose 3/4".

• 1 x "T" connector 3/4".

• 2 x 3/4 " connectors for tubing.

• 2 x Net Pots.

• Clay pellets 10# bag.

• 2, Rockwool cubes. 6"x6".

• Water-pump 264gph.

• 5 feet of 3/4" flexible plastic tubing.

• 1, end cap 3/4" for tube.

• 1 x 1/4" connectors.

• 4 feet 1/4" spaghetti tubing.

• 1 x pack of 1 gph-pressure compensating drippers

• 1, Bottle PH up.

• 1, Bottle PH down.

- Air pump.

- 12 Feet, air tubing.

- 1pk, air stones.

Preparing The Material

In 2 of the buckets, drill a three-quarter" hole, two inches from the base and In the final bucket, drill a 3/4" hole, one inch from the base (ideally, this would be your reservoir bucket). Proceed to insert rubber-grommets inside each of the three buckets.

Phase One

Take the five-foot piece of three-quarter" plastic hose and cut it in half. Insert a three-quarter" connector to 1 end of each piece of the hose. Connect both pieces of hose with the "T" connector. Insert "T" connector into grommet of reservoir bucket. Now that you have grommets and connectors on your hose and buckets, connect the other two buckets to the main reservoir. Your main reservoir will now be centralized in your system.

Phase Two

Fill a separate 5-gallon bucket with water and test pH levels using a pH tester kit. You may need to use your pH up or pH down to adjust your levels accordingly.

Once pH levels are optimal, you can dump your water into the buckets. The water level should equalize quickly. With the 5′ length of plastic-tubing, attach one end to the submersible water-pump, and then attach the end-cap to the remaining end.

With the one-quarter" hole puncher tool, make a hole on each side of the tubing about halfway down the length and insert 1/4″ connectors. Cut the 4′ spaghetti tubing in half fit each piece to one of the 1/4″ connectors. To the open end of spaghetti, tubing attaches a pressure compensating dripper.

Phase Three

Insert the substrate baskets into the 2 outer buckets and then fill about halfway with the clay pellets. Submerge your Rockwool cube into basket center and fill the basket up to the top of the cube with more pellets.

Phase Four

Cut the 12′ of air-tubing into equal dimensions. The total number of required lengths will vary depending on the available number of air outlets on your pump.

Attach each piece of tube to the pump, and to the open ends of your tubes attach air stones.

Put ends of air tubes with air stones into the reservoir-bucket. DO NOT PUTPUMP INTO BUCKET. Place next to the reservoir and plugin. watch the bubbles and have an iced tea.

Phase Five

Put the submersible water-pump inside the reservoir-bucket. Be sure to position your tubing between the 2 planter buckets and then stake the spaghetti hoses as well as drippers into the Rockwool. Ensure that before turning on your water pump, make sure it is completely submerged in water.

If you need to add more water, make sure you adjust the pH before adding it to your reservoir. Now plug in your water pump and watch your garden grow.

CONCLUSION

There are less disadvantages than there are advantages, but the downside is that those disadvantages are really strong. It's a high level of commitment so don't be fooled by thinking there's nearly double the upsides than there are downsides. Depending how committed you are to trying aeroponics, it could set you back a few hundred dollars for a quality aeroponic system. If that doesn't work out, you could have one expensive mistake on your hands.

That being said, it is a high-risk high-reward scenario because when the system is controlled to perfection, you will get a higher quality of crops at a faster production rate and much healthier plants than many other growing methods because of the 24/7 oxygen and nutrient supply to the plant roots providing full nourishment throughout the growing cycle.